HOMEBOOK

www.visualmusic.it

HomeBook
45 unicum graphics

from original images of HomeArt
programs (1986-1991)
by Pietro Grossi
*<autom@tedVisuaL1.0> software
by Sergio Maltagliati

*autom@tedVisuaL is a software
which generates always different
graphical variations. It is based on
HomeArt's Q.Basic source code.

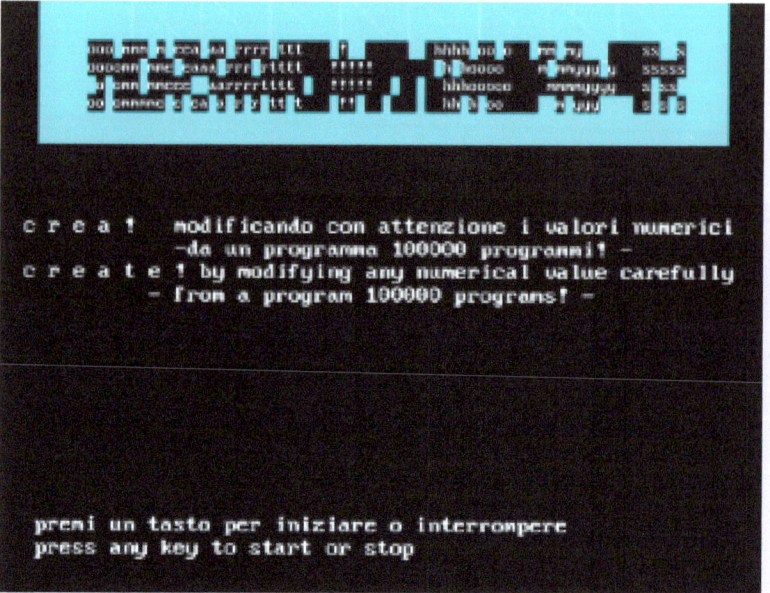

PIETRO GROSSI (1917-2002). He has not limited his work to the musical world, but also engaged in contemporary art. In the eighties he was working on new forms of artistic production oriented toward the use of personal computers in the visual arts. Grossi started to develop visual elaborations created on a personal computer with programs provided with "self-decision making" and that works out the concept of HomeArt (1986), by way of the personal computer, raises the artistic aspirations and potential latent in each one of us to the highest level of autonomous decision making conceivable today, and the idea of personal artistic expression(...). Grossi has always been interested in every form of artistic expression. The last step of his HomeArt, is the creation of a series of unicum books, electronically produced and symbolically called HomeBooks (1991): each work is completely different from the others, thanks to the strong flexibility of the digital means.
Sergio Maltagliati will continue this project creating autom@tedVisuaL software in 2012.-Wikipedia-

HomeBook 45 "unicum grafici"

PIETRO GROSSI (1917-2002) pioniere della musica
elettronica e computer music, negli anni
80 estende le sue ricerche al campo della grafica
(seguendo i medesimi principi usati per
la musica), con i progetti di HomeArt (1986) e di
una "editoria variabile" HomeBook (1991).
Questo ultimo progetto consiste in una serie di
libri prodotti elettronicamente, in modo da
assicurare l'unicità grafica di ogni copia. Sergio
Maltagliati continuerà questo lavoro progettando il
software autom@tedVisuaL che, partendo da
immagini di HomeArt (1986-1991) genera una
sequenza sempre diversa di innumerevoli
variazioni grafiche. Il software è basato sul codice
dei programmi originali di HomeArt nel linguaggio
Q.Basic. Le immagini sono destinate ad essere
inserite in libri (o e-books) completando il
progetto HomeBook teorizzato da Pietro Grossi.
La prima versione di autom@tedVisuaL, ha
prodotto 45 unicum grafici.

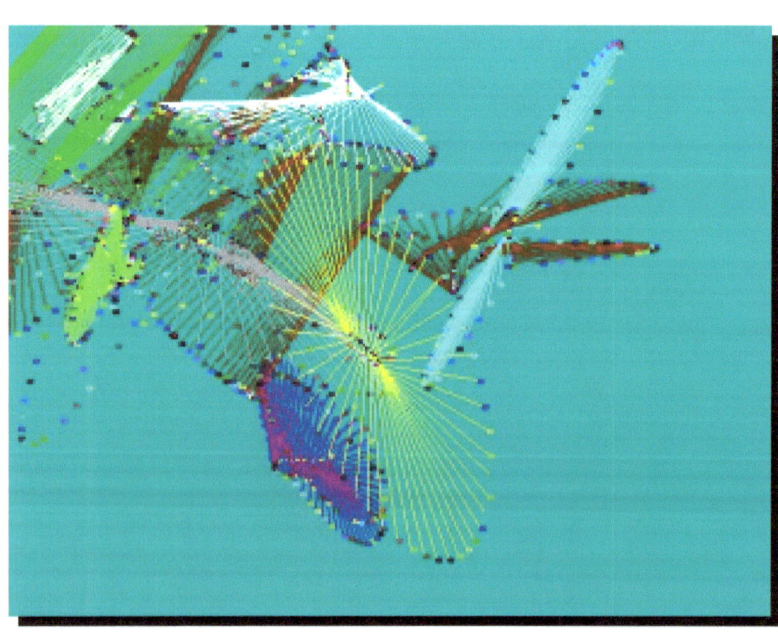

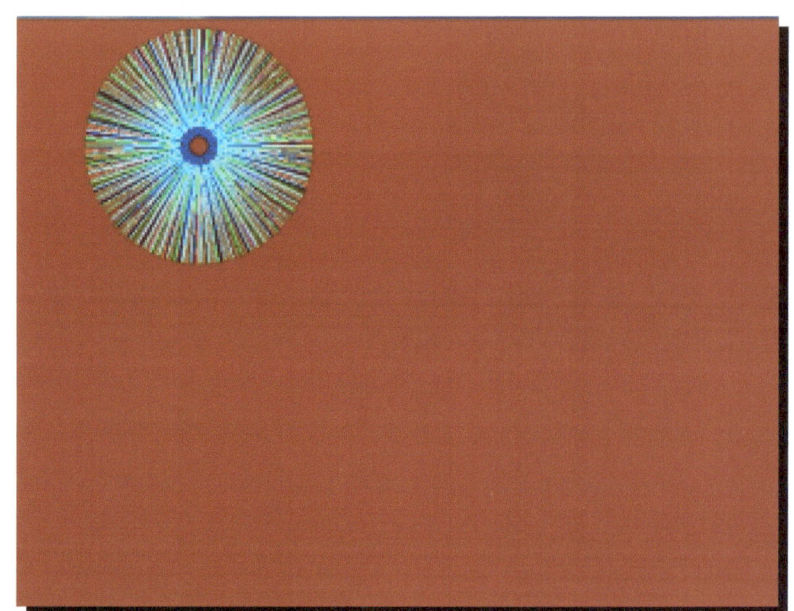

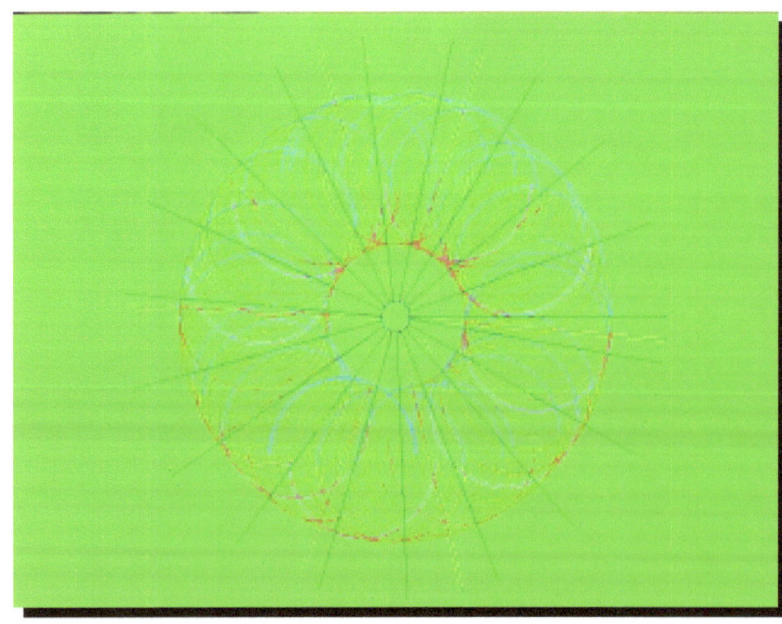

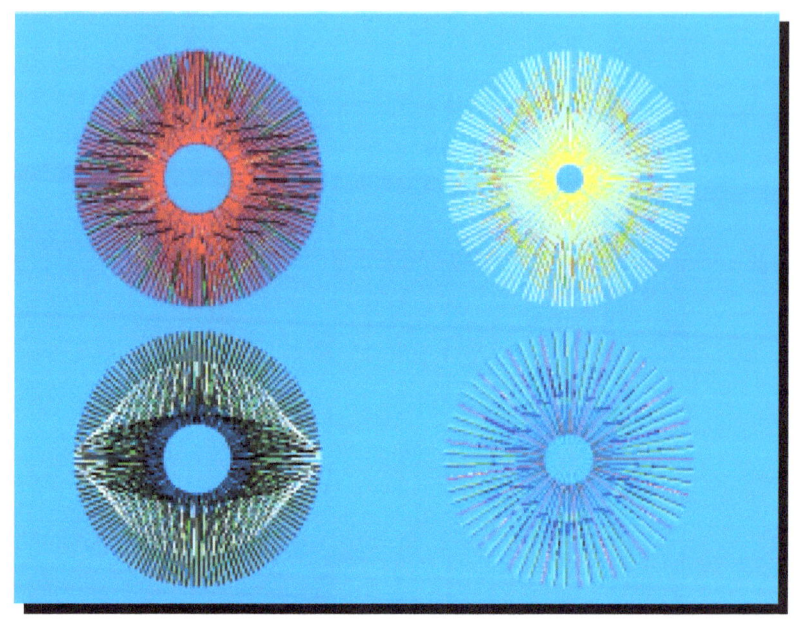
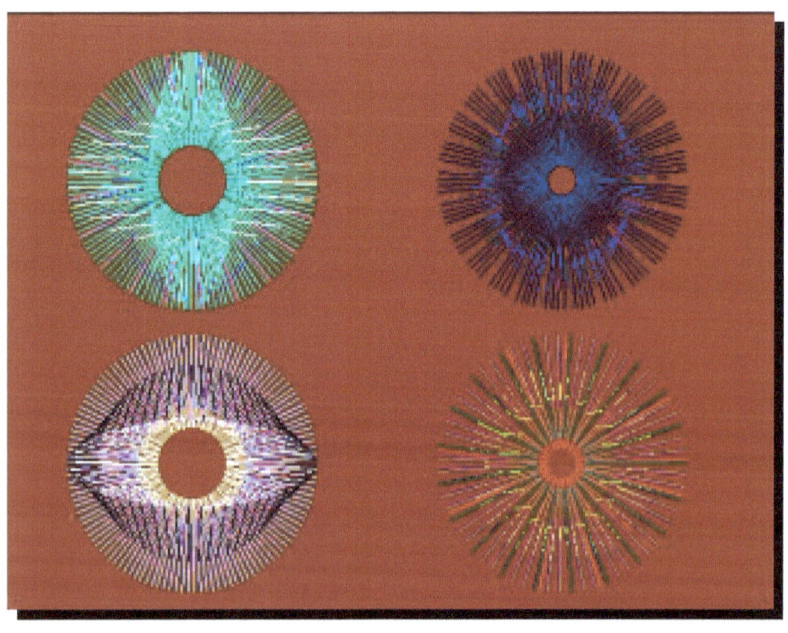

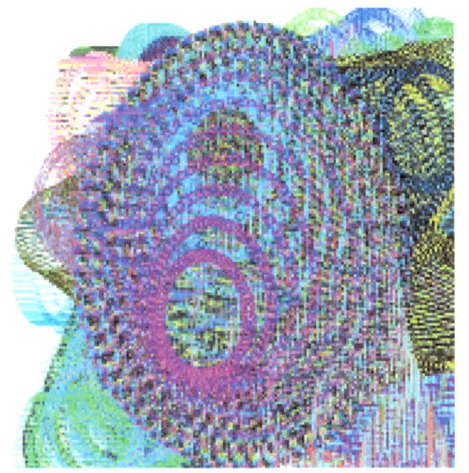

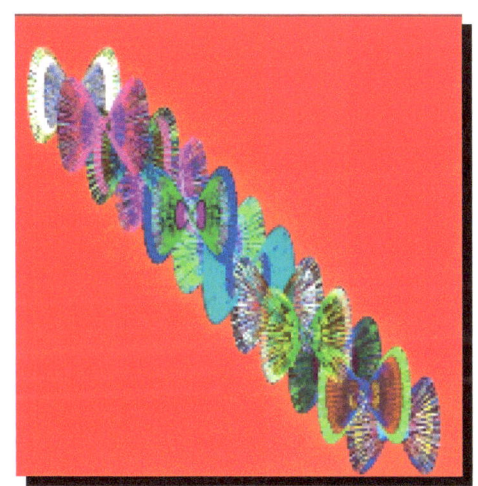

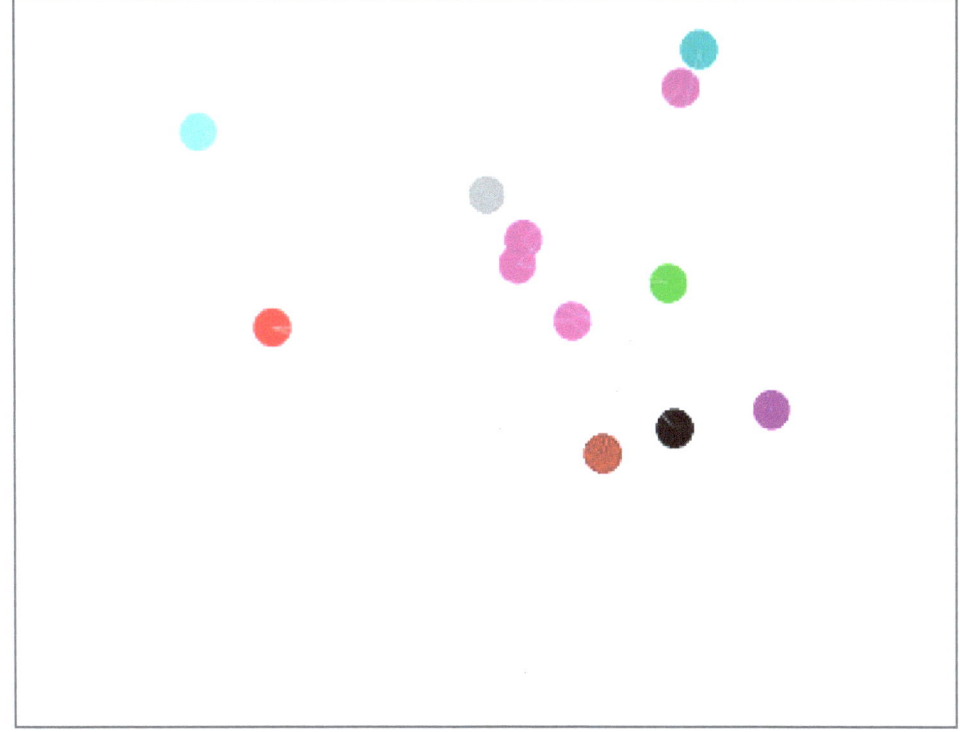

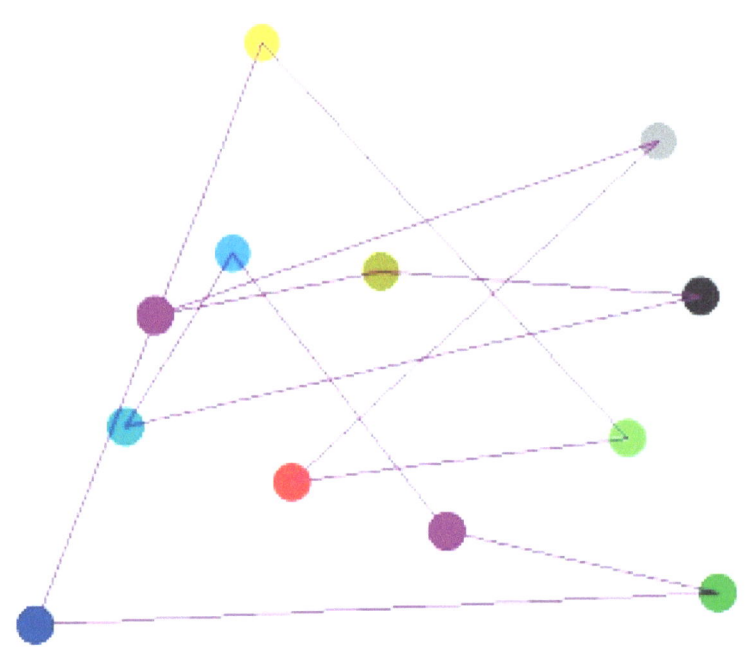

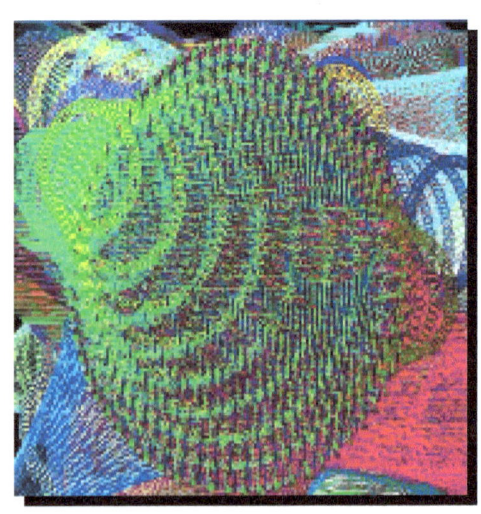

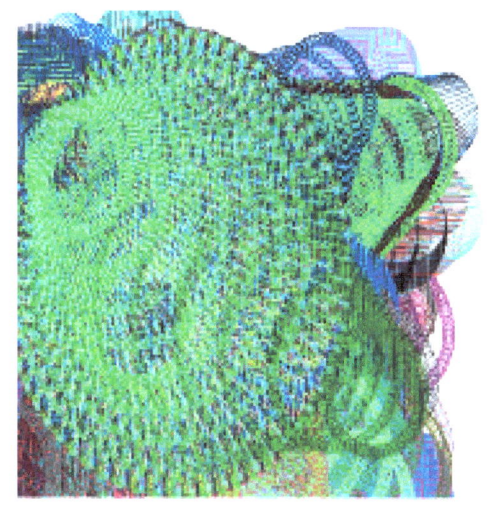

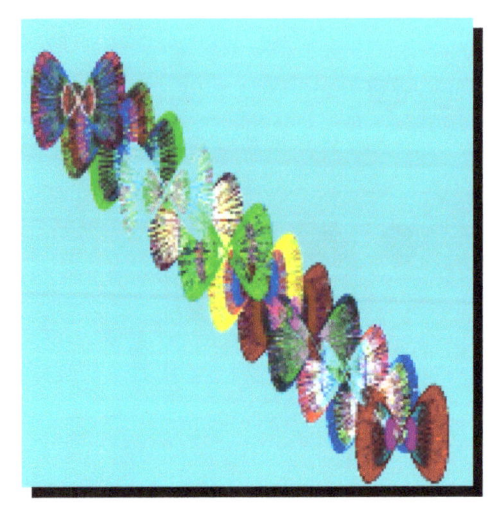
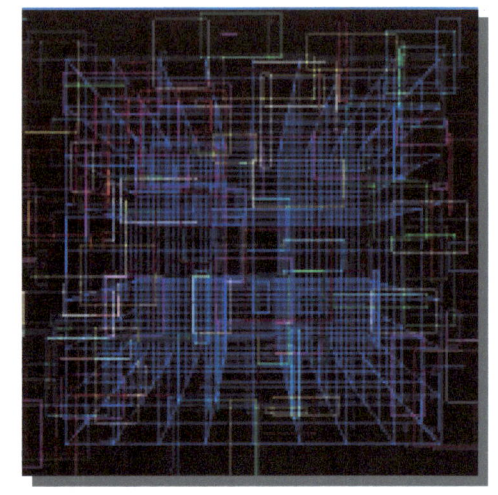

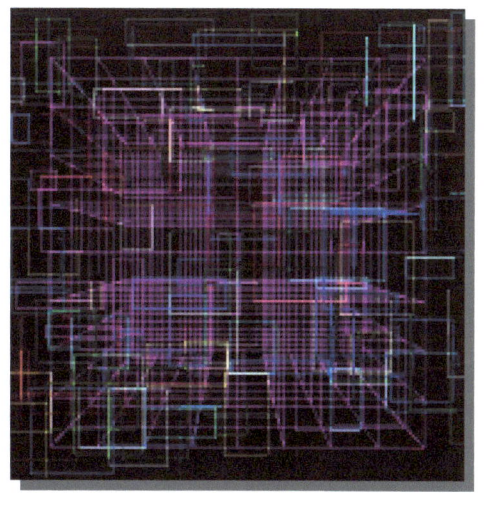

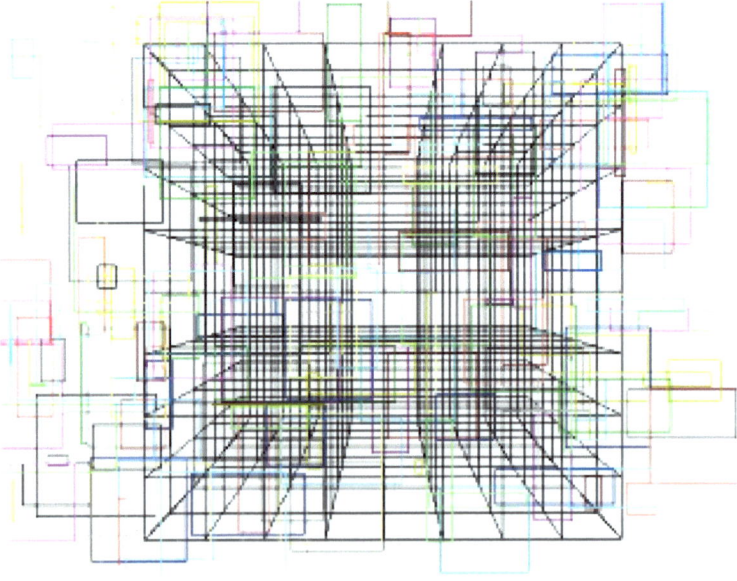

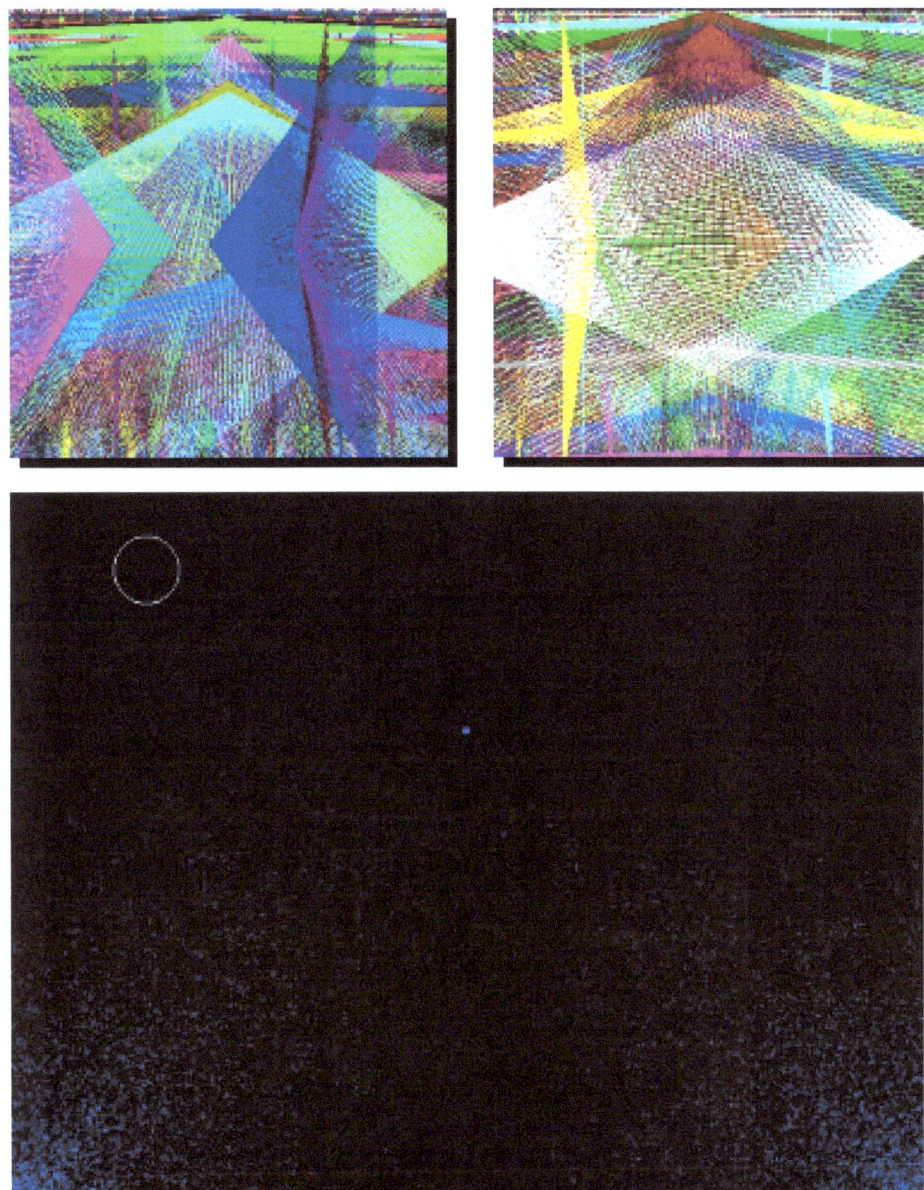

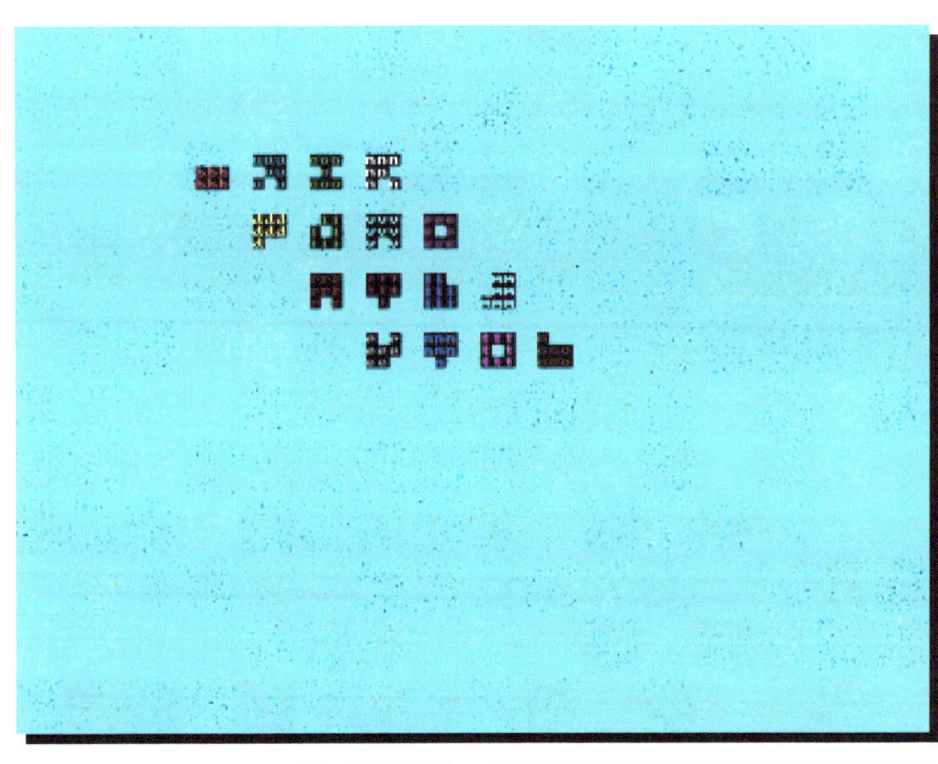

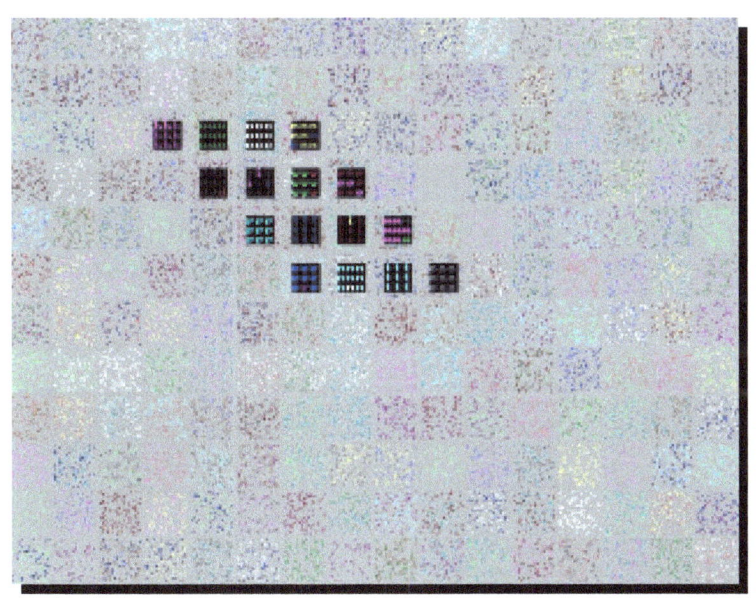

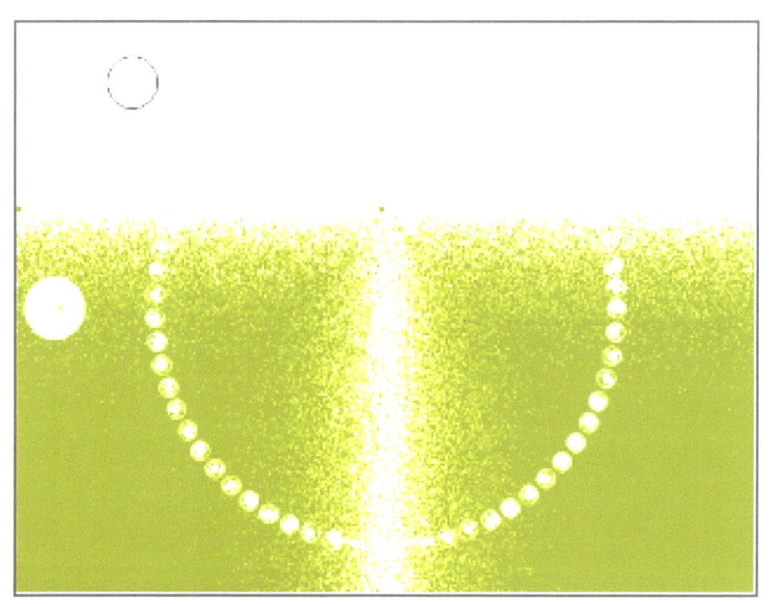

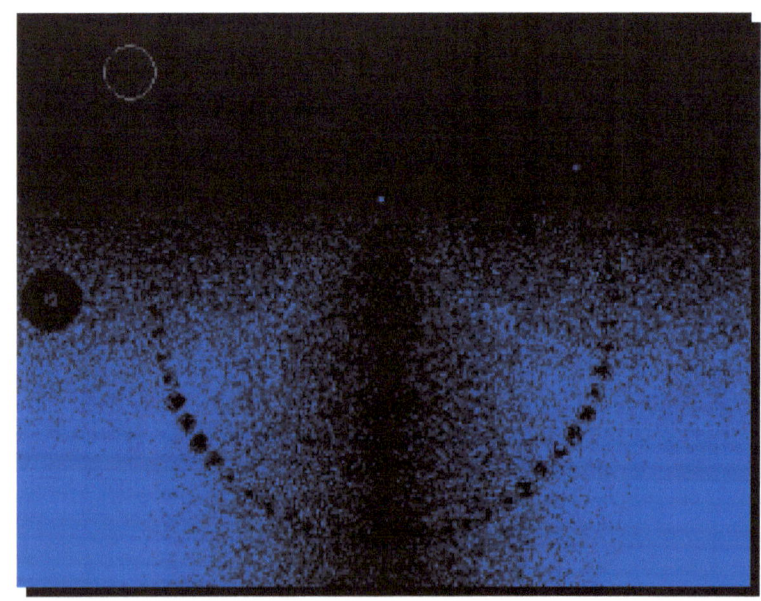

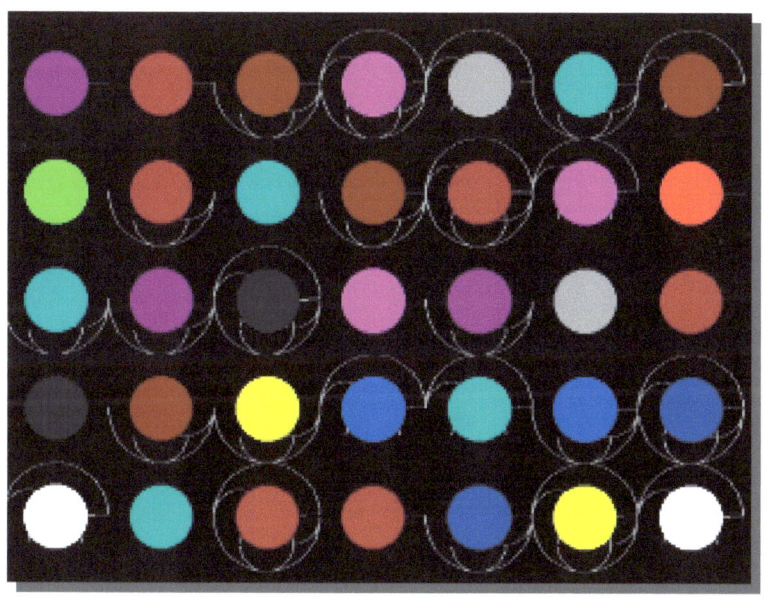

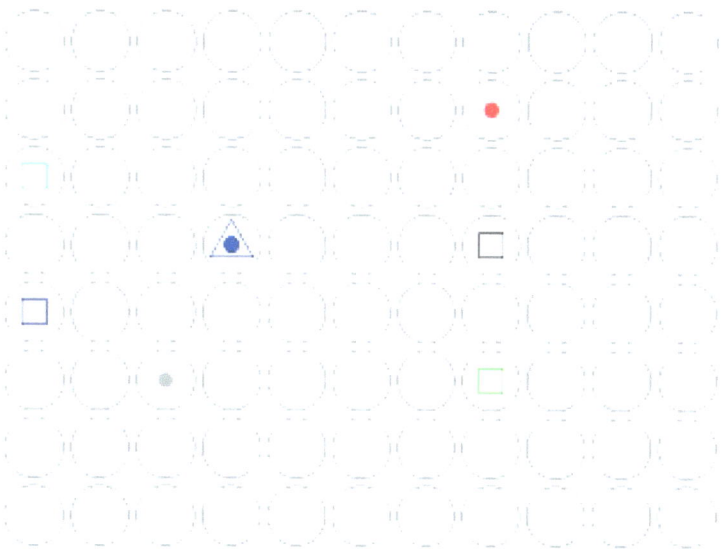

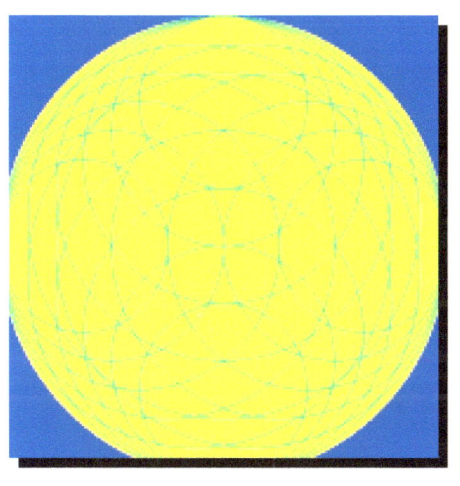

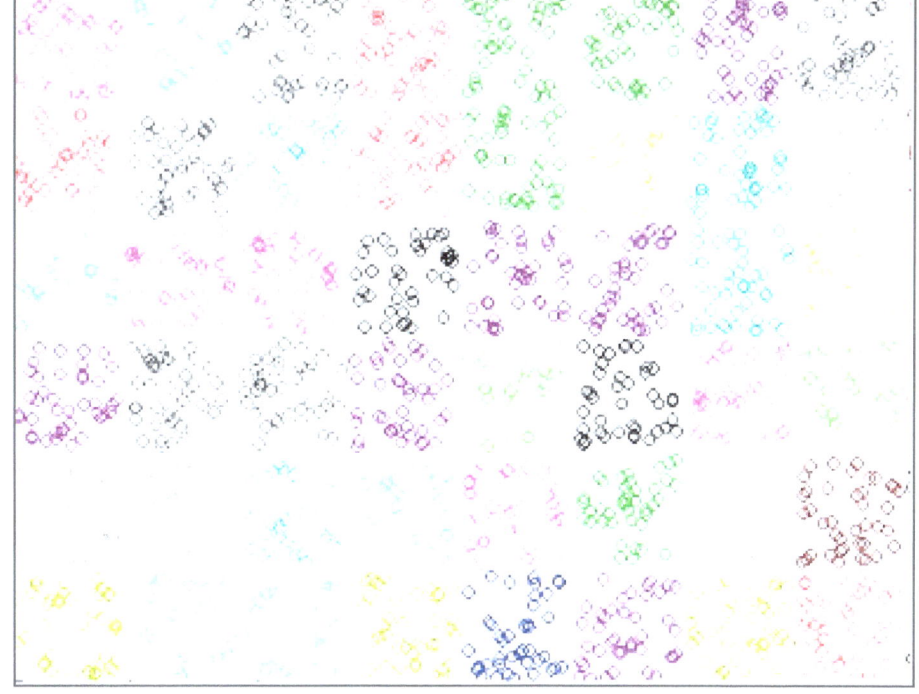

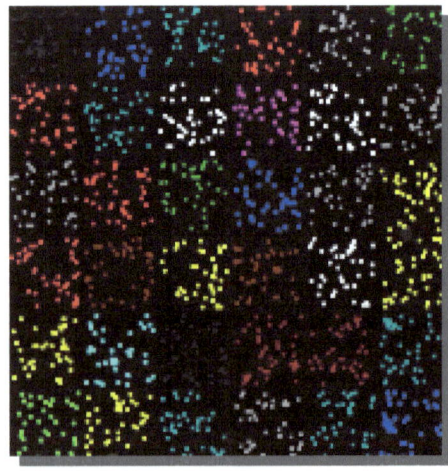

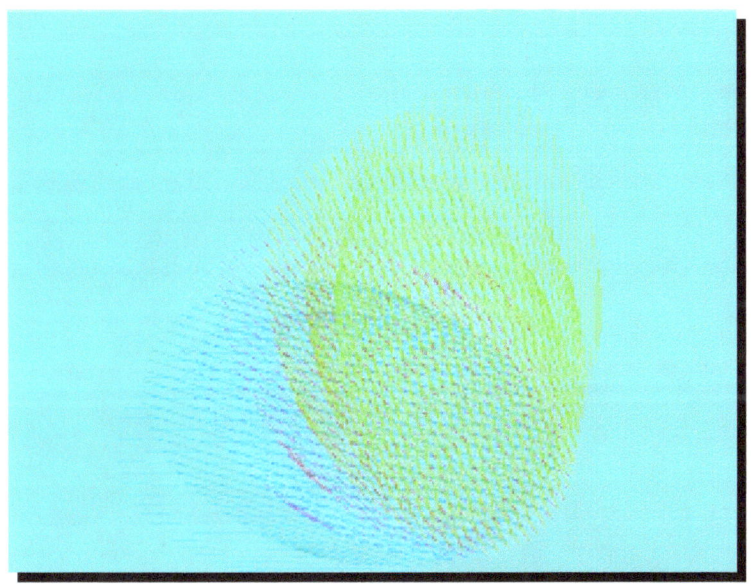

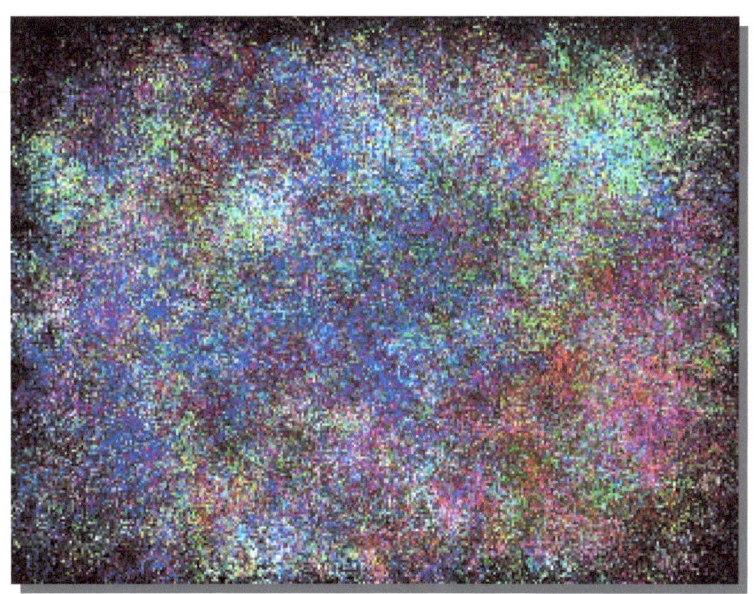

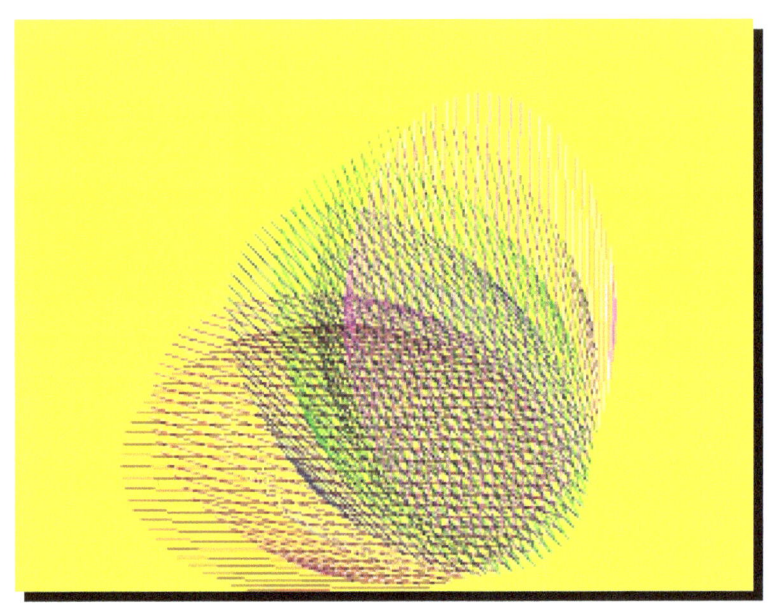

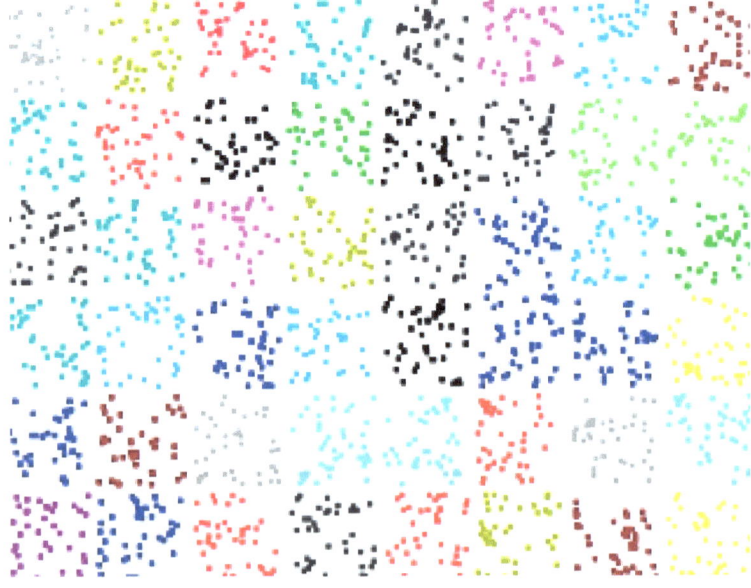

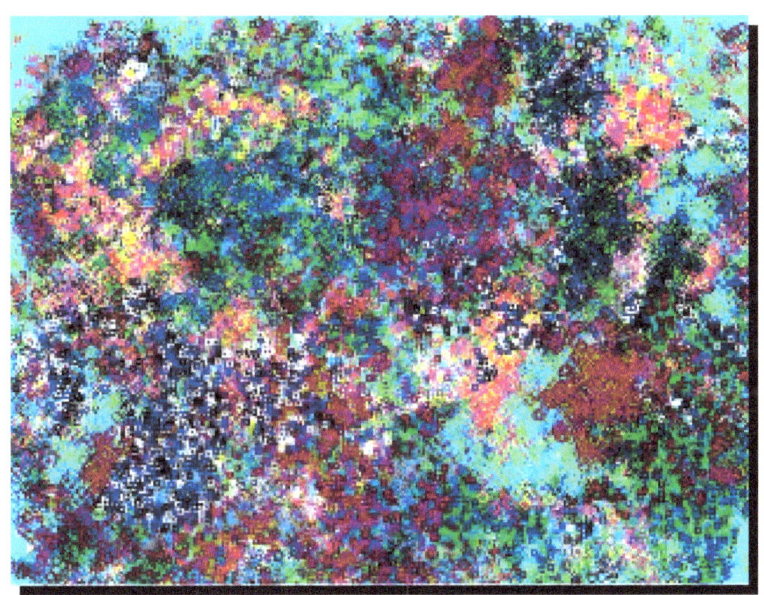

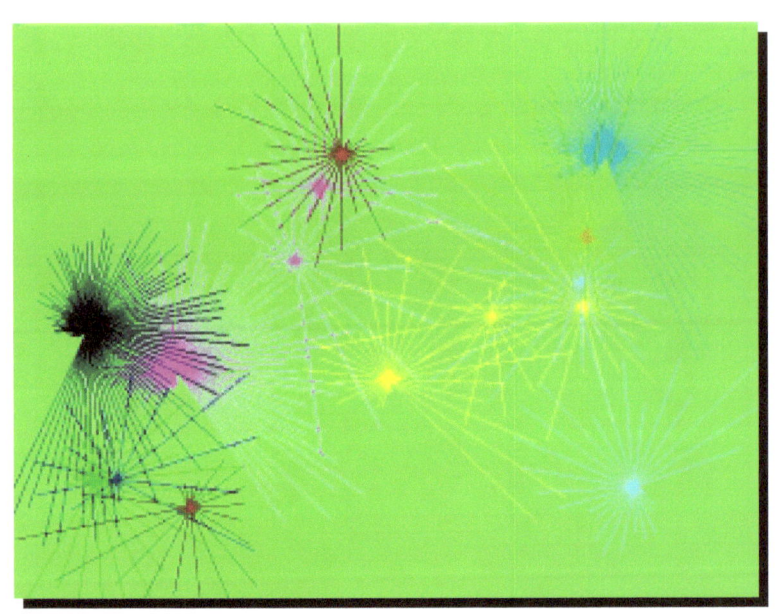

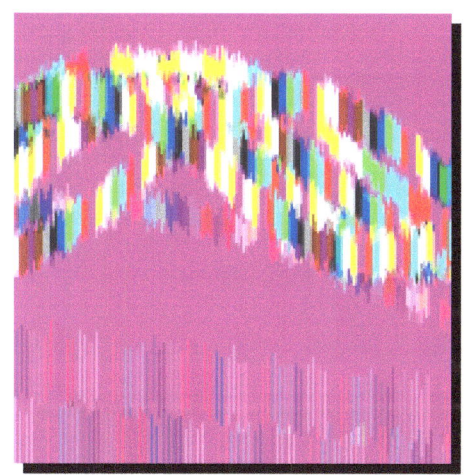

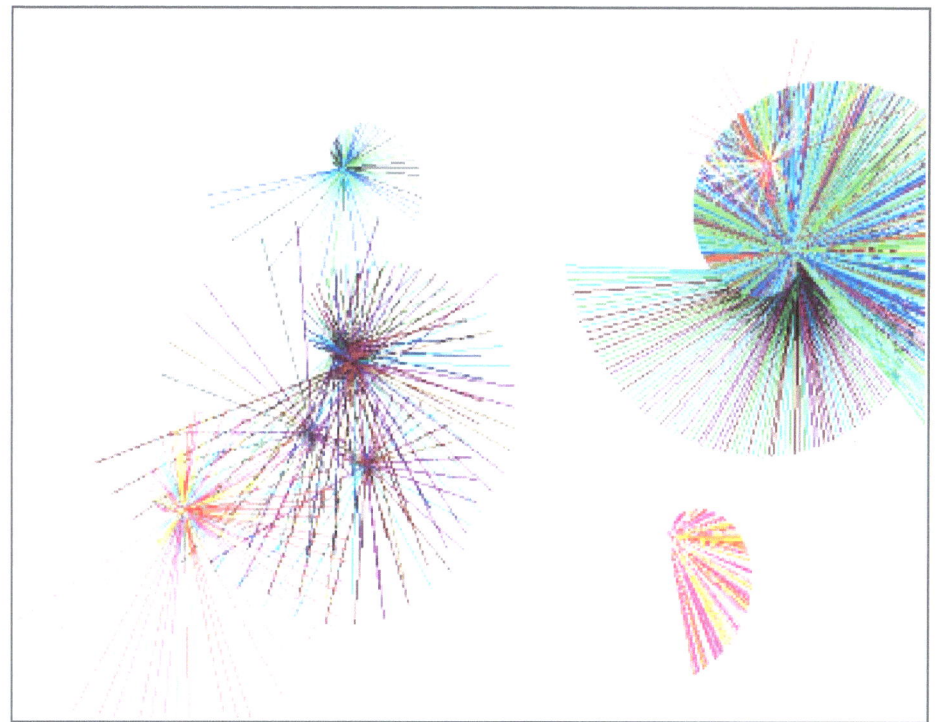

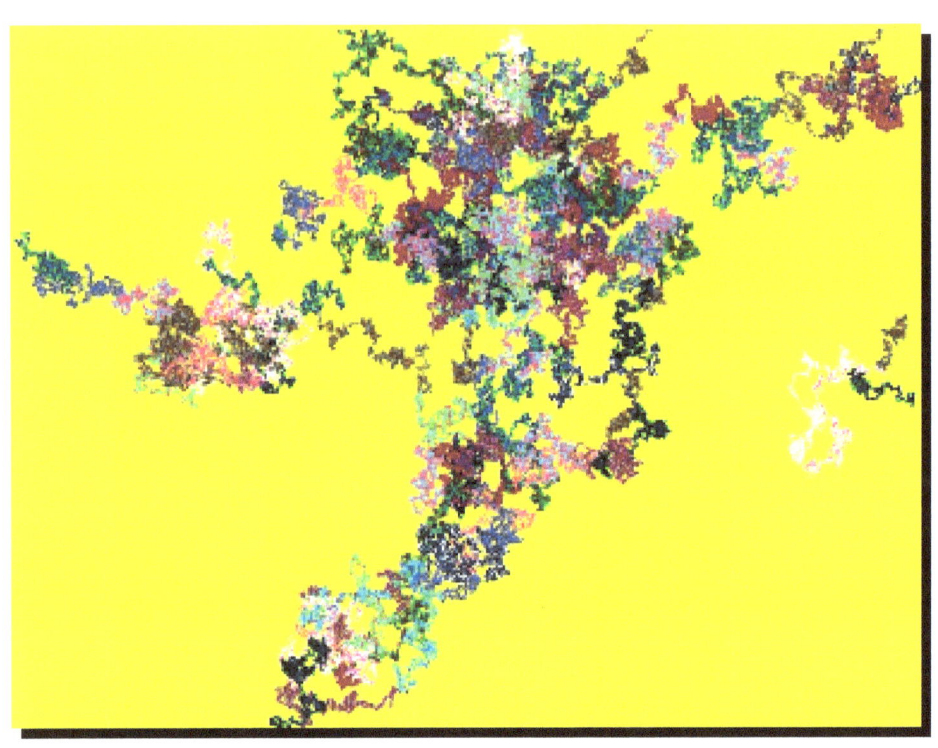

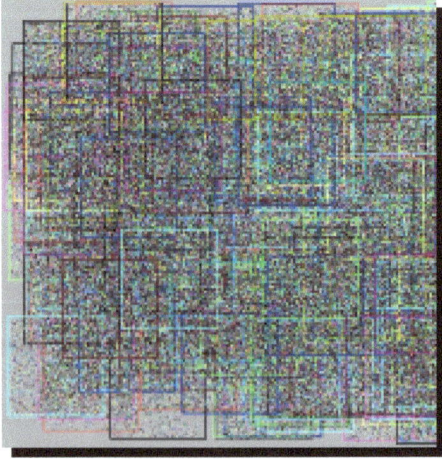

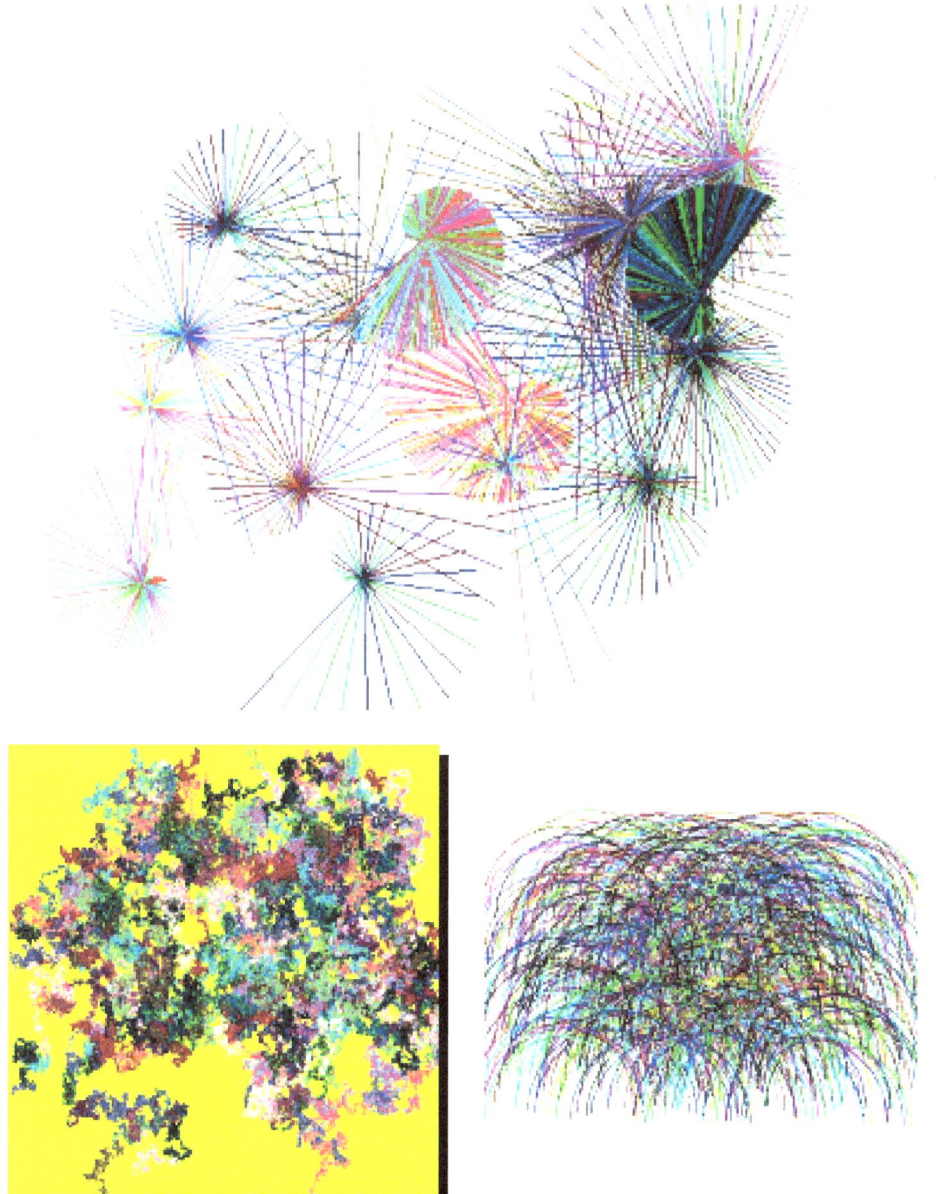

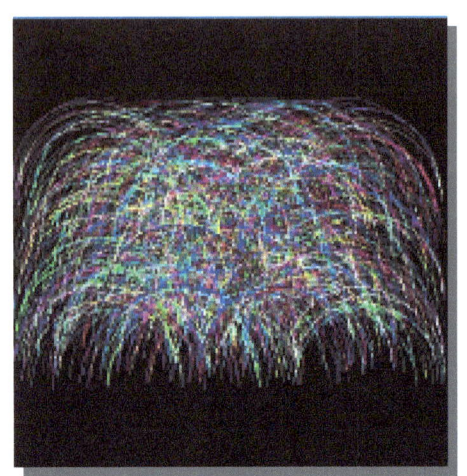

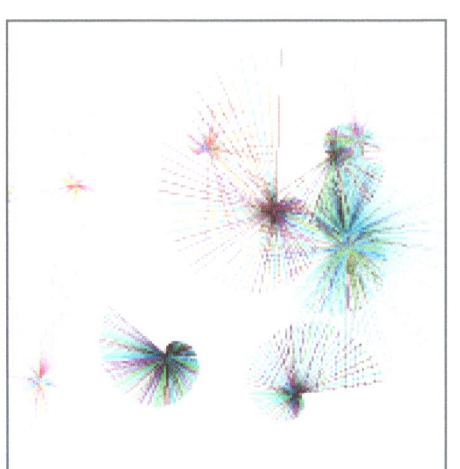

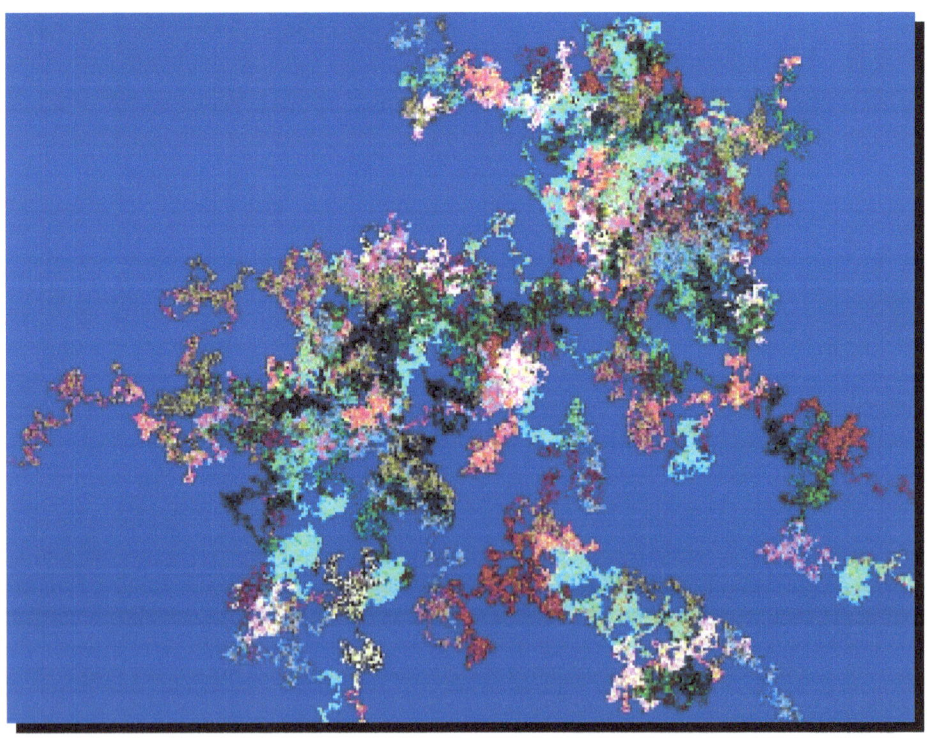

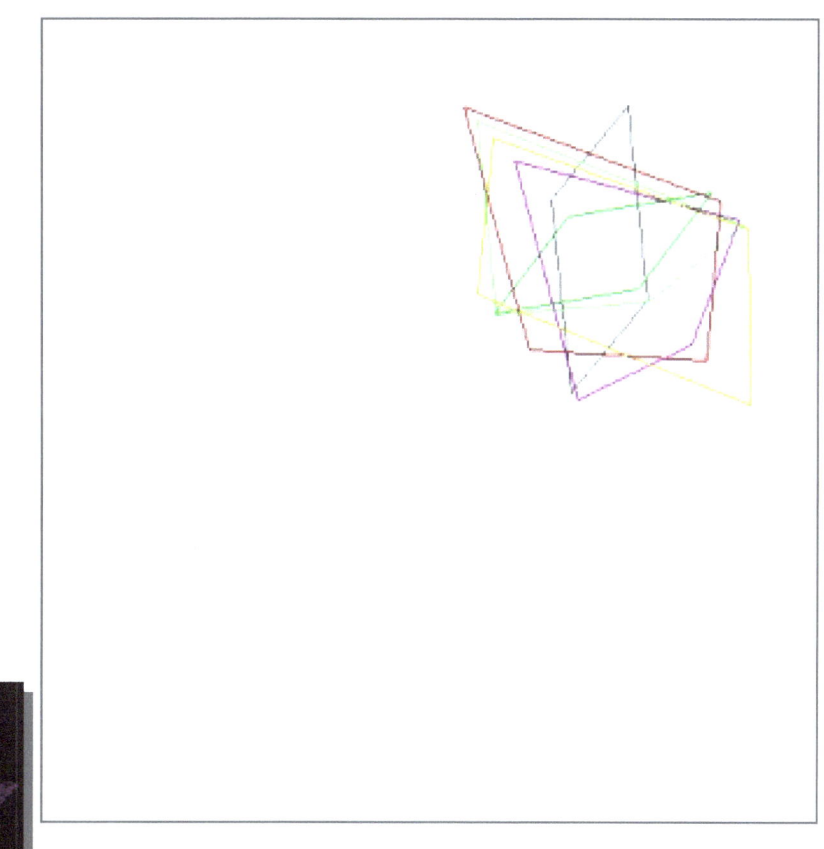

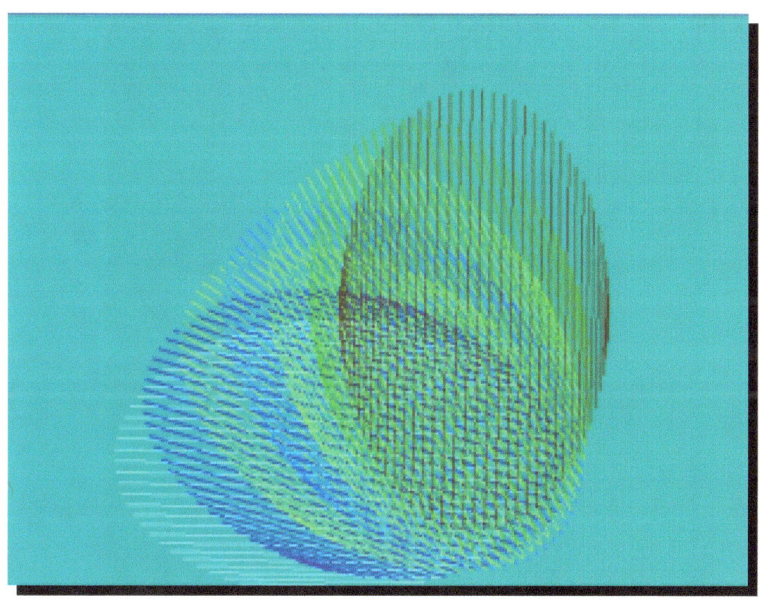

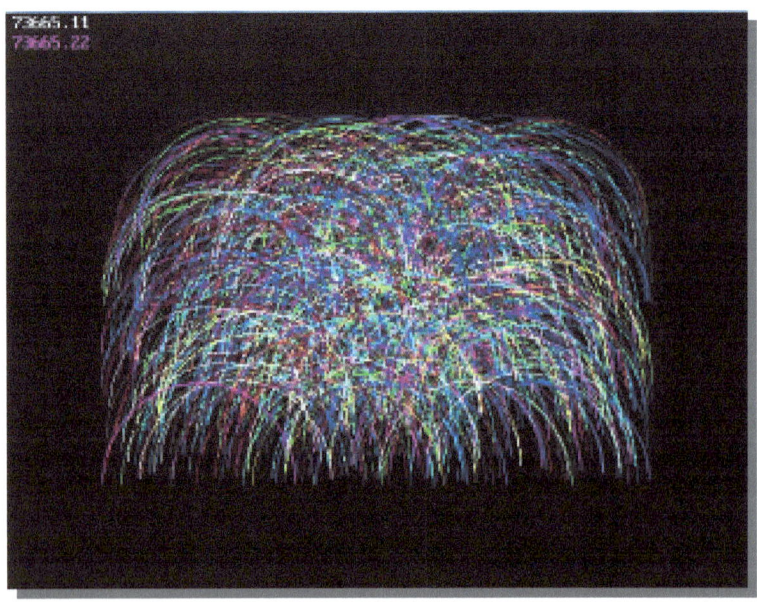

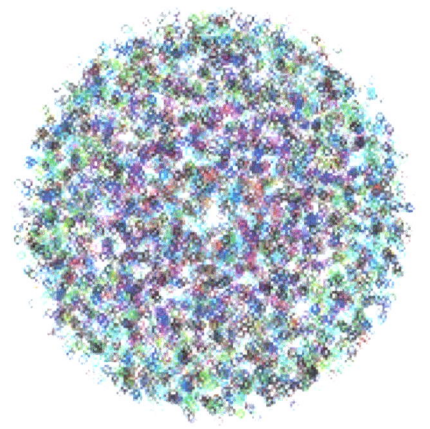

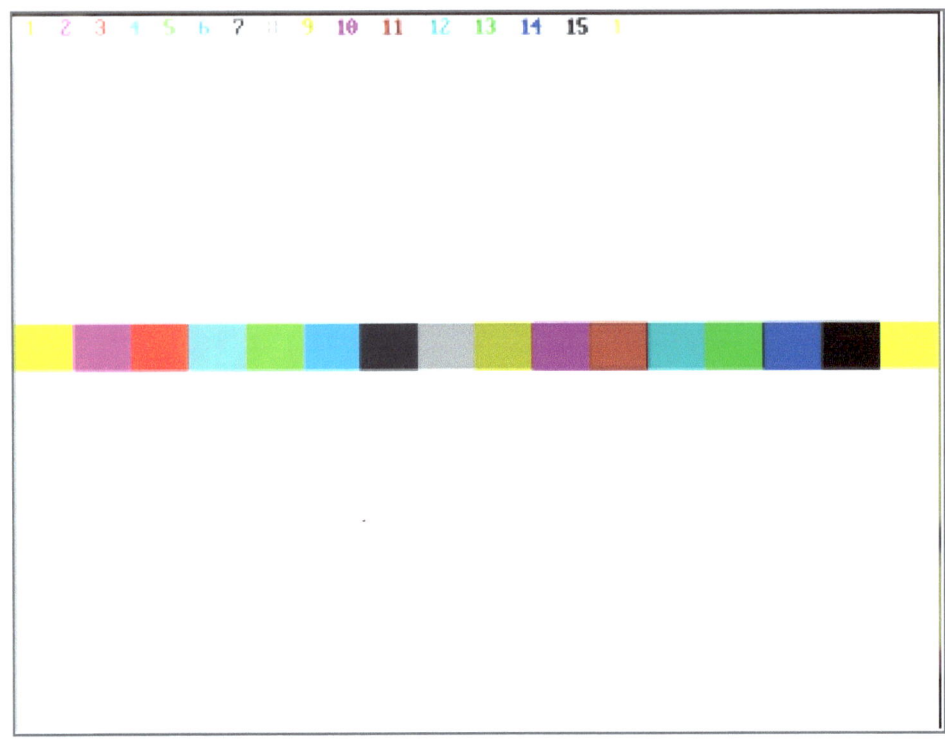

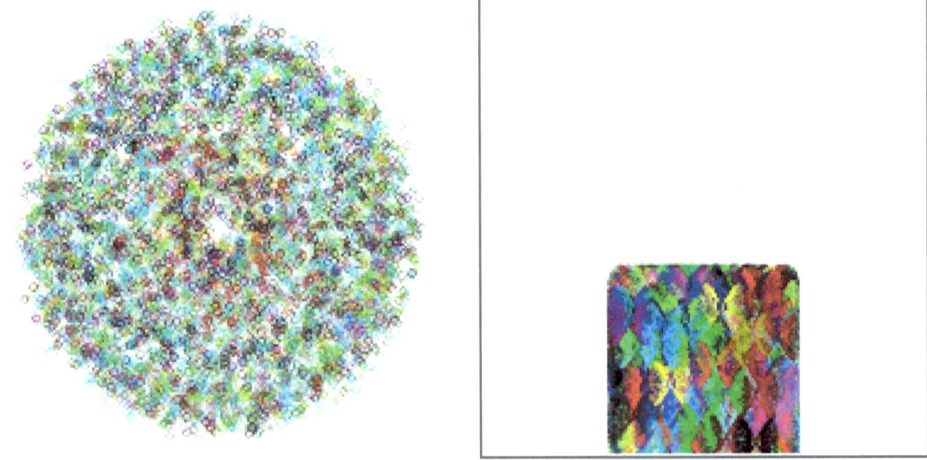

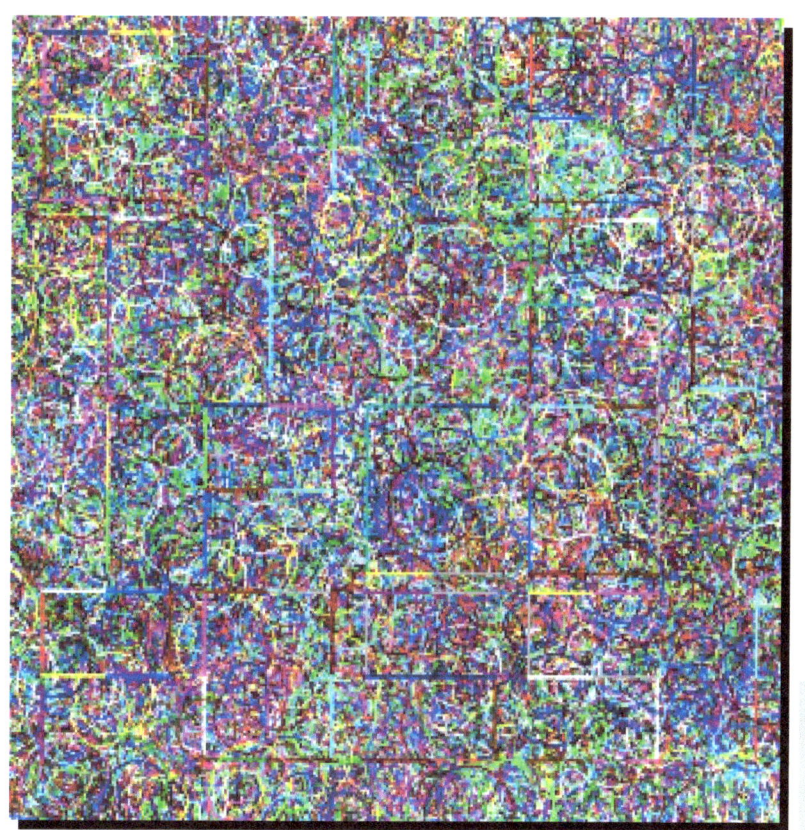

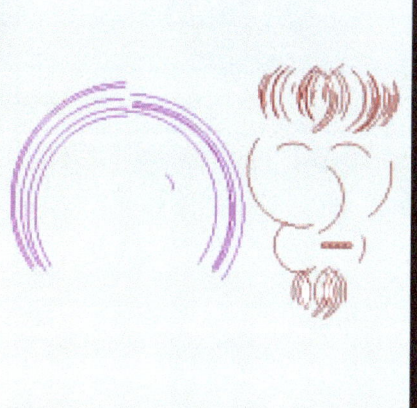

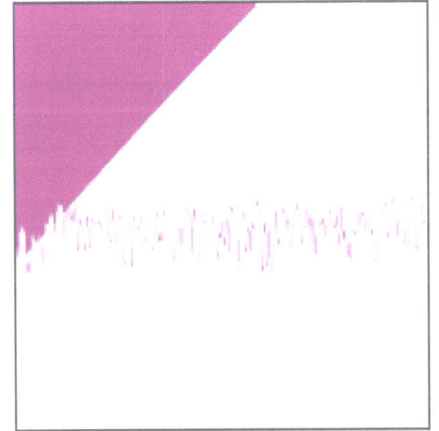

```
h    o    n    e    a       rt        !              ooo      n n    y      s s
h   oo    n e eaa  r r  ttt       ! !          hhhh       n n   yy      s  s
h  ho omn n ee e aarrr  r  t      !!!           h  oo      n n  yy       s ss
 hhh oo o n n e    aaa rr   tt     !          h h ooo o   n    yy


  w w  e  e  et t      ho   o  n n e e   a r t  t      !! ! !
    ee e ee  tt     hh hhooooonnnn eeeaaa  r  tt       !!  !!
w w   w eeeeee          h ooo   n n e a a rr rt t     !!!!!!! !
   w     e ttt   h  o        ee a   rt     !
```

Press any key to continue

Sergio Maltagliati - Pietro Grossi (2001) *Foto by Paola Zucchello*

45 "Unicum Graphics". The images are proposed through <autom@tedVisuaL> software from experiences of HomeArt programs designed by Pietro Grossi in the '80s, written in the language BBC Basic with computer Acorn Archimedes A310. This program can be configured to create random multiple visual variations, starting from a simple visual cell. It generates a new and original visual composition each time the play button is clicked. These graphics are going to be sammled into the HomeBooks (also available as e-books), a unique kind of book, which Pietro Grossi planned in 1991.

Visu@lMusic/HomeArt
www.visualmusic.it

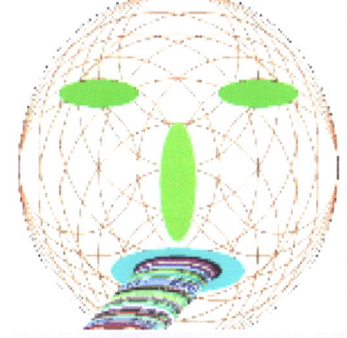

HOMEBOOK

(2012)

visualmusic.it

www.visualmusic.it

www.ingramcontent.com/pod-product-compliance
Lightning Source LLC
Chambersburg PA
CBHW051056180526
45172CB00002B/664